How to Write a Book to Benefit Your Clients & Your Therapy Practice

ASHLEY & CHRISTOPHER BRUCE

Find us At the Exhibitor Table!!

This special edition of the book was published for the 2020 FMHCA Conference. The Bruce Law Firm is an exhibitor for the conference and the Welcome Reception sponsor. Come find us in the hallway so that we can meet you and get your therapy practice listed on our state wide referral website (there is no cost for this) www.StayMarriedFlorida.com, and discuss setting up a time to interview you for our video and podcast series which you can leverage to promote your practice. We also have more copies of this book there in case you want to give one to a colleague, as well as free copies of our law firm's divorce books which can serve as a resource to you and your clients.

How to Write a Book to Benefit Your Clients & Your Therapy Practice

TABLE OF CONTENTS

ACKNOWLEDGEMENTS

Thank you to our parents, Chrissy, Bernice, Russell, and Spencer. Your continued love, guidance, and encouragement makes us the world's luckiest children and has put us in the position of accomplishing anything we set our mind to achieving.

We are also especially grateful to those in the mental health profession who have trusted the attorneys of the Bruce Law Firm to help meet the marital and family law needs of their clients, while also helping our law firm's clients move on from the difficult experience of divorce (and sometimes avoid divorce completely through couples therapy). This book is for you!

LEGAL DISCLAIMER

Figures a book written by a lawyer would come with a legal disclaimer. Yeah, this is one of those.

This book is written by a lawyer but is not meant to provide legal advice. I encourage you to consult your ethics rules and utilize common sense and good judgment before following any of the strategies in this book. And always consult an attorney who is familiar with the facts and circumstances of your situation before taking legal action. (And if you are reading this book looking for legal strategies, you are reading the wrong book… but we do have some books on the law at www.DivorceInformationBooks.com…).

INTRODUCTION

On most days when I go to work in my law firm, I want to thank my lucky stars because I feel incredibly fortunate. This is because we have a steady flow of clients whom we actually enjoy helping. And this allows our firm to provide a nice life for my family, and the families of all of our other attorney and paralegal team members.

But it wasn't always such smooth sailing. Earlier in my career, I at times became frustrated. Not all of my client work was satisfying. And not all of my clients were capable of paying for professional services in a manner that made for a stable business. This led to stress, burnout, and at times just made the job "not fun." Don't get me wrong, I always felt fortunate to be an attorney, but my practice just was not as fulfilling as it is now.

This all started to change as I started to think hard about what might make me happier in my law practice. After thinking things over, and considering the advice of several of my mentors, I came to the solution. It wasn't rocket science. I just needed to attract more of the types of clients that I enjoyed working with. For me, these were women married to abusive men (mostly because I felt these clients would have their lives improved by the divorce and they generally are more pleasant people to work with).

So, having identified my "ideal client" I sent out on getting more of them. I didn't really know how to do this, but I got lucky and figured it out by accident. Right about the time I was trying to answer the "how do I market to my ideal client" question I got a book in the mail from a local probate lawyer. He was about 10 years further into his career than I was, and he had sent me a book about some sort of boring legal topic that was actually very important for his law practice. I looked at the book, then looked at his website and saw that (1) he had written another book and (2) his firm had 4-5 lawyers (which gave me the impression that his marketing was working). I figured then and there that I'd just copy what this attorney did and write a book and maybe I'd have enough of my ideal clients one day to have a 4-5 lawyer law firm too.

Well, now five years and several published books later, I am no longer an employee at a law firm working for other lawyers. I have a multi lawyer law firm of my own. Obviously, me writing a few books didn't do all of that (*thank you by the way to everyone who has mentored me and trusted me to handle their divorce and family law referrals*), but it didn't hurt.

What writing the books for my ideal clients did do, however, was force me to take an even deeper look into the types of clients who really made me happy and how I could do a better job of helping them as much as possible. While writing the books, I had to hyper-focus on the most important needs of my ideal clients. And as I redefined what was most important to them, I also came to a few realizations on things I needed to change in my law firm to serve these clients better.

At the end of all of this "book writing stuff" I felt like I was much better equipped to help the clients I wanted to help the most, and I think that confidence has played a large part in the ability of the Bruce Law Firm to attract the clients we have.

And then there is the part where the potential clients and referral sources of the firm know I'm the lawyer who "wrote the book" on how to divorce a controlling, manipulative, narcissistic husband. For the most part, we don't have to do any "selling" when people interview myself or our firm's other lawyers. They already assume we know how to solve their specific legal problem.

So, I think I know what you are thinking. It probably goes something along the lines of *"Well that sounds great, but are you kidding me! I don't have time to write a book."*

I get it. Writing a book can seem overwhelming. It can also be time and effort intensive (the first one I wrote took over 150 hours and more than a year from start to finish). **But it doesn't have to be this way**. If you go through the process that I break down for you I feel you can complete a solid book that helps both your clients and your practice with 3 to 5 hours of focused attention.

Further, with the ease of self-publishing (kdp.amazon.com), the availability of internet "freelancer" help communities (upwork.com and fivrr.com), and cheap and reliable transcription apps that you can download to your phone (rev.com) you can write your book without actually writing anything and get the entire project done for less than $100.

Although writing a book can sound like a huge undertaking, I'll show you that it really isn't all that hard to do. I tend to guess that if someone told you how 3 to 5 hours of your time and less than $100 could allow you to better help clients, and get more clients, you'd do it in a heartbeat. That's why you should keep reading and write your own book!

Ashley & Christopher Bruce
West Palm Beach, Florida

Other Resources Designed to Help You (and Your Clients)

Before we go any further, we wanted to make a quick mention of books we've written in case you want to check any of them out as examples of what you can do. All of our books are available for free download at www.DivorceInformationBooks.com. These books are free and include the *Women's Guide for Getting Organized for Divorce, How to Divorce Your Controlling, Manipulative, Narcissistic Husband*, our guide on *How to Find & Hire Your Divorce Lawyer*, and *Control Your Difficult Divorce*, our comprehensive divorce strategy guide. You or your clients are welcome to utilize these resources, and there is an option when downloading a book to request us to send you (or your clients) a hard copy by mail.

Also, because it is our belief that the real best divorce is the divorce that didn't have to happen, the Bruce Law Firm developed and supports www.StayMarriedFlorida.com, a website devoted to helping couples build, have, and keep healthy relationships. The website has articles, podcast interviews, and a growing directory of extremely talented results-driven therapists. If you are a therapist and would like to be on the website, please reach out to us at cbruce@brucepa.com or (561) 810-0170.

Part 1: Why to Write and the Easy Way To Figure Out What Goes in the Book

Why Should You Care? (Advantages of Writing a Book)

There are multiple advantages to writing a book. I've highlighted those that I felt to be the most important to me.

Helps you focus on what you really enjoy doing: a book that is effective from both a practical and marketing perspective will usually be focused on solving a narrow and unique problem that you, as the professional, are capable of solving for your clients. I have found that the entire exercise that we will go through on how to write a book forced me to really assess what I enjoyed the most about my law practice. This allowed me to determine the types of issues that I most enjoy helping clients solve.

For me, this was an eye opener. As I went through the book writing process, I realized I was most passionate about representing women who are married to controlling or manipulative men (often narcissist or sociopathic personalities). Before I wrote the book, I knew in the back of my mind that I was most fulfilled by handling these types of divorce cases, but the book writing process helped crystallize what I enjoyed most in my law practice. This in turn has allowed me to create a professional practice that I enjoy.

Helps you focus on who you enjoy working with: just as the process of writing a book can help you discover the subject matter that you enjoy the most in your practice, it can also help you identify the types of clients that you most enjoy helping. While not all of our clients are always going to be our ideal clients, going through and identifying who it is you prefer to help makes it easier to ultimately have a business that is predominantly focused on serving clients that you really enjoy helping.

Expands who you can help: I feel that most therapists, like most attorneys, pursue their profession because they want to help people. Unfortunately, there is not enough time in the day to help everyone. By writing a book that focuses on solving a narrow problem that you know how to help your ideal type of client solve, you are able to expand the universe of people you help from those people you meet with in your office to anyone who can download your book on the Internet.

Creates/expands your "authority/celebrity" status: it is fairly difficult for the average potential client to question the qualifications of a therapist who "wrote the book" on a particular subject area. Most people know that writing a book is a huge accomplishment and assume that anyone who writes a book on a particular subject knows what they are talking about.

From a marketing perspective, this makes it easier to become known as the "expert", especially for solving a niche problem, which in turn allows your practice to still prosper in an otherwise flooded market, sometimes partially from referrals from competitors. I feel my book, *How to Divorce Your Controlling, Manipulative, Narcissistic Husband* helps accomplish this for my law practice (which has six lawyers as of this writing!). This book helps women feel like I know how to solve their problem of divorcing a difficult man, and makes it easier for my law firm to stand out from the probably 1,000 other divorce lawyers in South Florida. I sometimes even get referrals from other divorce lawyers who know I focus on this niche area because they don't like handling these particular types of cases.

Justifies the rates that you charge: many of us can feel uncomfortable when we tell clients how much we charge to do what we do. When you write a narrowly focused book, you are going to find that clients are less prone to hiring you based on price, as they know they are hiring an expert who knows how to help them solve what is, to them, a very important problem. This allows you to charge appropriately in your practice. Money is not everything, but you should be compensated fairly. The book helps assure that happens.

What Should You Write About?

A book can be about anything. There are no rules. You can write a book full of poems, a personal memoir, or a book about upside-down clowns eating purple cheesecake on the moon. It's all up to you.

That said…if you are writing the book to help your clients and your practice, there are some guidelines I suggest you follow to make the book effective. I reference some of my books in this section and below as examples. If you want a copy of any of my books for yourself (or your clients) they are available for free download at www.divorceinformationbooks.com. Or just email me at cbruce@brucepa.com and I'll email or mail any of the books to you.

Anyway, in terms of selecting the topic, here is what I suggest you do:

HOW TO WRITE A BOOK TO BENEFIT YOUR PRACTICE

<u>**Write for your ideal client:**</u> for the book to have the most impact, you should be writing it for your ideal client. If you have several types of ideal clients, then just pick one and write the book for that one client. If your book "speaks to the masses" then it will probably "speak to no one". You can always rework the material to appeal to the other clients later.

If you do not know who your ideal client is, then now is the time to find out. My suggestion is you take a notebook and a pen and put yourself in a quiet place. Try to think of the 5 to 10 times over the last year or two that you have felt incredibly accomplished as a professional and write down the details of the types of clients that were associated with those feelings of accomplishment. You might find that there are several trends that emerge in terms of the types of people you enjoyed helping the most. My suggestion is you write the book for that person. Obviously, you want to be realistic about whether or not your ideal client represents a client that can form the basis of an economically viable therapy practice.

Oh, and in case you're wondering, you will likely find that a narrowly focused book helping your ideal client will still attract other people into your business. I am no longer surprised that a fair amount of men download my women's divorce books and ultimately become my clients.

Example Applied: For me, I realized that as an attorney, I felt most accomplished when helping women leave marriages from very difficult and controlling men. I realized that I felt by taking on these representations (which are very challenging) that I would not only be helping a client through a legal process (the divorce), but I would also help them towards having the opportunity to completely reshape their life. And for many, that means actually having a chance at happiness once the divorce is over. So, when I went to write my last book, I decided that it would be for women who are considering divorce from a controlling or intimidating husband.

Write the book to solve a narrow problem for your ideal client: I feel the most effective books are also going to have a narrow topic. You will be best served by writing your book on the subject of solving an important problem that you can help your ideal client solve. If you have been in practice a while, all you might have to do is think back in time to what seemed like an important way you helped previous clients that represent your ideal client type. Keep the subject of the book concise. Doing so will make the book more effective and will keep you more focused. You can always write other books later.

**Example Applied:** for my ideal client (a woman considering divorce from a controlling/manipulative/narcissistic type husband) I focused my book on helping the client understand the most important things they should know leading up to starting the divorce. In many ways, the book is focused on helping my ideal type of client mentally prepare for the divorce process. I stick mostly to this one subject even though the book could have been much more in-depth and covered things like what happens in a divorce, or how the divorce laws work, etc. (since I have been writing books for a while now, I have other books that focus on those subjects).

How to Write the Book

If you love the feeling of staring at a blank page on the computer and using the keyboard to fill it with words, then by all means, feel free to just start writing! I suggest you don't do that though. I did it with my first book and it took forever. Since I have an accounting degree and am not especially fond of writing, I found the process incredibly laborious although the end result was rewarding. Don't do what I did the first time around. It takes too long and won't be fun.

The next time I decided to write a book I thought to myself: I have a spouse, two young children, clients to help, and a business to run. How do I make something that is very helpful and effective and in way less time? As that thought was passing, I went back to client work and dictated off a set of instructions to my paralegal for work on a client matter.

That's when the light bulb went off. I was going to dictate (record yourself talking) the next book instead of writing it. So, I got to work and the next book was done in a few hours instead of a year.

I will cover the technology on how to do all of this in the next part of this series. For now though, all you really need to know is the cost of transcription is about a dollar a minute and the app you can get on your phone for the dictation is free. For most of you, the book won't be much longer than 60 to 90 minutes of you talking.

The best way to approach writing the book (regardless of whether you end up dictating out the words or writing them on the computer) is to plan the content and structure of the book in advance. Below I give you a fairly simple formula for doing this with references to my *Divorce Your Controlling Husband* book as an example. If you intend to dictate out your book, all you need to do is write down a few bullet points under each of the main points that I go over below and you'll be prepared.

Book Writing Formula

Below is the way I suggest you organize the content of the book. My suggestion is you can make this very simple. For the book to be helpful it does not need to be hundreds of pages long. All you need to do is get 3 to 5 bullet points for each of the topics below and you will be ready to either dictate or write your book.

Here's the formula:

#1: <u>Identify the problem that needs solving</u>: In the first part of the book you need to identify the problem that you want to solve for your ideal client. You can probably do this in one brief chapter like I did in the *"Identify the Predator"* chapter of my *Divorce Your Controlling Husband* book (by the way, you should feel free to download a free copy of the book or request one from my by email cbruce@brucepa.com to use as an example when doing this writing). When you are "identifying the problem" you should do your best to do so from the viewpoint of your ideal client. It is optimal when your ideal client reads your description of "the problem" and thinks to themselves that you really understand them and their situation. They should read the chapter and say "this author knows me."

#2: Help the reader realize they can be part of the solution: therapy, like divorce law, doesn't happen in a bubble. Clients have to be part of the process of solving "the problem". The next part of the book should help your ideal client feel hope that "they can do it." You want to inspire them that they can be a big part of solving "the problem" even though they might otherwise feel they cannot "do it". Make them believe that solving their problem is possible and they are part of the solution (this must be true because your practice is built around solving their problems while interacting with your clients…right…? I do this in the *"Realize You Have the Power to Change"* chapter of my *Divorce Your Controlling Husband* book.

#3: Identify why solving "the problem" is critical: you should then get into highlighting the benefits of solving your ideal client's "problem". Make it clear why it is worth your ideal client to even bother solving "the problem". I tried to do this in the *"Define The Life You Want (Your Vision)"* chapter of my *Divorce Your Controlling Husband* book, but could have done a better job. If I were to rewrite this book, I would have written a more descriptive chapter of how my female client could have had a much better life

12

once she was able to experience the peace and unlimited potential that can come from escaping the day to day anxiety and torment caused by a toxic and emotionally abusive relationship.

#4 Identify the pitfalls/challenges that come with trying to solve the problem: most "big problems" worth solving are not solved simply. You should bring out this fact in the book by explaining some of the challenges associated with your ideal client solving "the problem". This helps give a more realistic view of what is going to be necessary to solve "the problem" and also leaves room to suggest why your ideal client might need some help (you) in solving their problem. I do this through the "*Get Realistic About How Your Husband Will Act During the Divorce*" chapter of my *Divorce Your Controlling Husband* book. Reading that chapter might give you some ideas.

#5: Explain what your ideal client can do now to get started in solving "the problem": although, ideally, your ideal clients will hire you to help them solve "the problem" I encourage you to devote at least one chapter (preferably two or three chapters) in the book to helping your ideal client understand things they can do, by themselves, to help them solve "the problem". I am not suggesting you should tell the client that they can solve "the problem" all by themselves. However, if you really think about it, there are probably certain ways your ideal client will be a part of solving "the problem", even if it is developing a certain mindset before hiring you. Write about those types of things. As an example, in my *Divorce Your Controlling Husband* book I do this through the following chapters: *"Keep Quiet: Don't Let Him Know What You're Planning"; "Get Organized for Divorce"; and "Plan Your Getaway"*.

#6: **Explain your role in solving the problem**: as you get closer to the end of the book you need to introduce how you or someone in your profession plays a part in helping your ideal client solve "the problem". Help the client understand how you or someone like you can help. Some people might market themselves, while others just explain how someone in their profession is helpful in solving "the problem" and let the fact that they wrote the book about solving "the problem" speak for itself (it would seem to be unlikely that someone would read your book and then start looking for other therapists without first considering you). I took the latter approach in the *"Find the Right Lawyer"* and *"Boundary Testing"* chapters of my *Divorce Your Controlling Husband* book.

#7: **Give next steps that can include contacting you**: my suggestion is you close out the book by helping your ideal client understand further resources they should consider reading/watching, and then make it easy for the reader to understand how they should go about contacting you. Remember that most people who are going to take the time to read a book about solving "the problem" might not necessarily be ready to solve "the problem". These people might want to learn more about "the problem" first. If you have other helpful materials about solving "the problem", such as a specific article on your website, or a YouTube video, you might consider including references to those resources in this chapter. Otherwise, you can direct the person to other helpful materials written by other people, or just give general advice for the "next steps". I have several different books on various aspects of divorce and divorce law, so I reference those resources as well as how to contact me in the *"Get Moving: Your Next Steps"* chapter of my *Divorce Your Controlling Husband* book.

#8: "About the author section": you should consider a section at the end of the book that gives more information about you. Through the "about the author" section you can highlight your experience in helping your ideal client (any maybe other client types) solve "the problem". I do this at the end of my book. My view is I highlight my expertise in this section and not so much directly in the main part of the book so if someone wants to learn more about my law firm, they can just read that section.

To reiterate, my suggestion is you should make a concise outline of the book content based on the eight sections above. All you need is 3-5 talking points for each section.

Don't make this more complicated than it needs to be. Otherwise, you'll never get the book project off the ground. You can always revise the book and do an updated edition later. I am a perfectionist as an attorney when I work on legal matters but realized that the only way to really make progress as a writer and marketer of legal services is to publish my drafts for the world to see and update those drafts later. Otherwise the book just remains a "draft" and nobody can benefit from it.

Again, just make 3-5 talking points for each of the sections listed above and that is all you need to form the basis for a book that will help your ideal clients learn how to better solve their biggest problems (which ideally they then hire you to help them solve).

Get Started

The most important thing to do is get started. Just do it. There is no better time than now. Otherwise this will never get done. Take this handout, get a notebook, and make your outline on the points above. Once you do that, you will be ready to dictate (speak out loud into a recording app on your phone) the content of your book.

Part 2: How to Write Your Book Without Actually Writing a Word

How to Write a Book Without Actually Writing: Rev.com

How do you write a book without actually writing anything?

To be honest, you will be writing, you just won't be the one doing the writing. A much more efficient way of writing and creating your own book is through a method called dictation. Dictation allows you to "speak your book" instead of typing out the words.

Dictation is probably much more common in the legal profession than in a therapy practice, but it is something that be used in a variety of professions to create content quickly.

When it comes to writing a book, dictating the first draft of the book through a dictation app like rev.com is incredibly easy and not expensive at all. It will dramatically speed up the time it takes to get the first draft done. Furthermore, if you are like me and the thought of sitting down and looking at an empty page on a computer feels daunting, a dictation app method of writing a book is the way to go!

Rev.com is simple. You download the app for free on your phone or iPad. Then you record yourself talking through the content of the book. After that, you upload the audio file and it is transcribed. Usually this takes place all within hours.

When I first started my legal career, transcription was very expensive and hard to outsource, but now it is exceptionally cheap. Rev.com costs $1 a minute if you want to have a human transcribe what you record. The cost goes down to 10 cents a minute if you want the transcription to be done through an automated computer program. The automation is not as accurate as a human doing the transcription, but it is one-tenth of the price. If the cost of doing this is a concern or your book is very long, this might be something worth thinking about.

If you don't like Rev.com, there are dozens of other transcription apps that basically do the same thing. These apps are all the same. You talk into a computer or your phone and make a recording of what you want the content of your book to be and someone else types out the actual words into a file. Then they email you the file. And voila, you have the first draft of your manuscript that might have otherwise taken you a year to write.

Revise The Book Using An Online Editor

Many people get intimidated about writing a book because of the cost of hiring an editor. When I was researching for an editor for my first book, I saw that some people would spend thousands of dollars to hire various editors to work on their project.

That might be fine if you want to have a New York Times bestseller. However, if your goal is to help as many people as possible by putting a book together on a topic that will really help them, then you don't need to go through all that. The first draft of your book does not need to be perfect.

All you need is something that looks professionally done and is 95% error free. Most people won't notice little errors anyway, and small grammatical issues will not detract from the help the book will be giving the readers. Further, over time you can always continue to edit the content once you have "first edition" complete.

There are ways to find affordable people to edit the book. My first book was close to 400 pages (*big overkill by the way, your first book doesn't need to be that long*) and I had an editor do an outstanding job of two rounds of edits for less than $1,000. I may have even found someone cheaper if I had taken more time to shop around, or if I only had one round of edits done.

Realistically, I think you could have an excellent book that's in the range of 35 to 70 pages, and could probably get someone to edit the transcription from Rev.com for a few hundred dollars or less. The cost of having this book edited was under $50.00.

When searching for someone to edit your book I recommend using freelancing websites like upwork.com. Upwork.com has a network of freelancers who do various projects including editing books that are in draft form.

To get started on upwork.com, you just need to create a free profile and job post. You'll want to add all of the details you are looking for in the description of your job post. If you decide to use Rev.com it would be good to add that in so that the freelancers applying know they need to have experience with that platform.

Here's a simple job description example:

I am searching for an editor to assist with my 70 page book. This person will need to download the manuscript from rev.com, edit the document, and send it to me when finished. Looking for someone who has editing experience, familiar with rev.com, and can turn around work efficiently. Please submit a proposal if you have experience and are interested in this opportunity! Thank you!

Once you hire someone you will have the writing/editing of the book complete within a few short weeks.

Cover Art Through Fivver/Upwork

Now it's time for the cover art!

When I wrote my first book, I spent close to $800 on having someone design the cover. It looked great, but later when I wrote my other five books, I had an equally great cover created for less than $100. I suggest doing something cheaper, simply because you can always get a better cover later. If you really want to treat yourself, spend more, but most people, beside yourself, will probably not notice the difference.

Another great website to hire freelancers is Fivver.com. This website is similar to upwork.com, except it has a lot of creative freelancers that are perfect for this kind of project.

When you look on Fivver.com, you will find people who specialize in creating book covers and do them very efficiently. You will also find many of the freelancers offer different package options as well. Whether you are looking to have someone create just the book cover, back of the book cover, book jacket, or all three you can choose an option that's right for you.

You will also want to have them create the cover as a PDF file as you will use this later when you (self) publish your book.

In addition to Fivver.com, you can also find a book cover designer on upwork.com. The major difference between these two websites is on Upwork you will create your own job post and invite freelancers to it. On fivver.com you search for a freelancer you want to use and purchase one of the packages they have available.

You can have the book cover created at the same time you are having someone prepare the edited version of the transcription for your book. The cover will probably get done quicker and then you will have something cool to look at. Fun, fun!

Now, onto how to actually create the book. All by yourself. Who knew you were a publisher?

(Self) Publishing: Kindle Direct Publishing

Years ago, to publish a book meant that you had to take your manuscript and send a bunch of stapled copies to all the publishing houses, mostly in New York.

You would then hire an agent to follow up with those publishing houses to see if the agent could convince any of them to actually publish what you had already written. Then you would wait. And wait. And wait. And wait some more. Then, if you got lucky, after more waiting, you might get a phone call where one of the publishers would agree to publish your book. After another year of more waiting and editing, your book might finally show up in a few bookstores.

Fortunately, times have changed and you don't have to do it this way anymore. Now, you can simply upload your book online. You'll upload your finished manuscript as one file and then update the book cover that as a separate file. With a click of a few buttons, you'll have an electronic version of your book all ready for you to review.

After a few more minutes of filling out information, which includes information to make your book available for sale on Amazon if you want to, your book is finished.

There will be about a day-long period where they approve everything, but I've never had a problem with that. Then you'll get an email that your book is approved, and at that point, you can order your own copies.

The copies are cheap. For my book that was in the range of 50 or 60 pages (the *How To Divorce Your Controlling, Manipulative, Narcissistic Husband* book) the copies are about $3 each after shipping.

All you have to do is choose how many copies of the book you want to order to give out to your clients and anyone else you have in mind. You'll be prompted to put in your credit card information and in a few days the books will show up at your office door.

Get Going On This Already!

Writing a book and getting it published is not rocket science and you can get it done for under a few hundred dollars with only five to ten hours of your own time involved in the production.

I encourage you to give this a try. I think you'll find as you go through the process that you'll feel more confident about yourself as a practitioner. In addition, you are doing an incredible service to the community by making it easy for people to get the information they need to solve very important personal challenges.

Further, once you get the book done, you can put it in electronic form and give it away for free. At that point, you're really helping people. Of course, this all makes for great marketing as well.

Part 3: How to Use Your Book to Attract Your Ideal Clients

Introduction

Once you have finished planning the book and writing the book, you should take a moment to congratulate yourself on being a published author. Congratulations!

However, you are not done yet. In order to provide the most help to the world, you need to get the books in the hands of the people who will benefit from them, as well as the people who can get the books into the hands of the people that will benefit from them. This process, which I like to call "marketing", serves a dual purpose. It helps you help people (*isn't this the reason you became a therapist?*), and also allows you to get more clients into your therapy practice. Which actually in turn, allows you to help more people. (A great cycle, isn't it!).

Most professionals, including therapists and lawyers (like me) are turned off by the idea of marketing. We went to school and received professional training to help people not to have to worry about "business stuff" like marketing. However, these marketing efforts are what allow us to help as many people as we can and is a big part of what will make your time and investment in your book worthwhile.

So there are several different strategies I have used personally to market the books that I have written. I have learned some of this through trial and error, and there is not a one size fits all approach here. There are several different tactics that I have covered below that will work for you.

The key here is to not get overwhelmed by all of the ways you can market. Just pick one of these ideas at first and run with it. I have tried to list the marketing strategies for your book in a manner from what is easiest to implement to more complicated. My hope is that you at least start with the first strategy and then eventually try one or two more.

I hope it goes without saying, but I am available to talk through any of these strategies with you. I have done everything below with the books that I have written for my law firm (if you have not read them yet, they are all available for free download at www.divorceinformationbooks.com) (I think most of you have a copy or two of my books, but if you would like me to mail any of them to you, or send you the e-book versions for your own use or distribution to any of your clients who might be in need, please do not be shy to ask, just send an email to cbruce@brucepa.com).

#1: Remember, you also have an e-book: Yes, you wrote a book. Yes, it should be printed and can be printed for likely less than $3 or $4 a copy from kdp.amazon.com and the other online self-publishing companies.

But don't forget, you also have an e-book. You can turn the manuscript of the book into a PDF file. In fact, you have to do this to make the e-book at least through Kindle Direct Publishing.

My point is you have a PDF file on your computer that has your book (and all of the helpful information in it) that can be sent to anyone you want to send it to. For $0. Just the time it takes to send an email. Your only investment in this method of book marketing is the time it takes to write an email and add the book as an attachment.

As you read the other strategies for marketing your book, do not forget that it doesn't have to be complicated. You can just email your book out to anyone you want to receive it including any current clients and referral sources. This does not have to be complicated or expensive. It can be as simple as this, which might be your preferred method if you are very early on in your practice or do not have a lot of resources to devote towards marketing.

Conveniences of sending an "e-book" aside, you do need to face the reality that many emails are ignored. And an e-book can be thrown out by clicking a button. Whereas people are less likely to throw out a hard copy of a book mailed to their office (which probably has very few books in it since a lot of practice resources are now in electronic form). A couple of dollars it costs to print out a book can be well worth it. It's not like you are going to be distributing hundreds of thousands of these things. For a few hundred dollars, you can probably print all the copies you will initially need. And that is probably worth the investment to you.

Book marketing strategy #2: Give your books to your current clients:

Who are the people who are most likely to be helped by your book? Your current clients of course. These are the people that are already trusting you to help them with improving their mental health. Obviously, this has to be done on a client by client basis, but if you feel the book would be helpful, give it to your clients. In fact, give them two, one for themselves and one for someone else they think could benefit from it.

Your current clients, who are likely to be very satisfied in working with you, are the people who are going to be most likely to refer people to your practice, so they should have a copy of this book. Also, you do not have to go out of your way to give the book to your current clients. Presumably they're in your office, so you can just hand them a copy at the end of the session. Boom. Bang. Instant delivery and no mailing costs. This is a great strategy and you should utilize it and definitely give them the second copy.

Book marketing strategy #3: Mail book to current and past referral sources:

Most mental health professionals have at least a handful of other professionals who refer to them on at least a periodic basis. These might be primary care physicians, other therapists with other specialties, or maybe even a few lawyers.

You should make a list of all of these people who I referred to you in the last several years and mail them a copy of your book with a letter briefly explaining the book and how you wanted them to have it. All of this will probably cost you $5 to $6 with the cost of postage by the time you have the book printed, but it is probably going to be well worth it. This will create a lot of buzz, and most of the people will end up keeping the books.

I did this when I published my first divorce book a few years back and sent it out to most of the lawyers and therapists that I know. It seems like most of the therapists gave the books to their clients, but the lawyers seem to be hoarders and I still get comments at lawyer events about how they have a divorce book on their shelf from me in their office, and sometimes even a snarky comment about what their spouse thinks of the fact that they have a divorce strategy book on the shelf in their office...

This is all very much worth the investment and I see this as an almost mandatory thing to do. After you send out the books by mail, probably two weeks later, you should follow up with a brief email that also attaches the e-book and encourages them to share it with anybody who might benefit from it.

If you're reading this and realize you do not have a list of your referral sources that is probably worthy of a whole another book topic. I very much urge you to make this list as it is the most important thing you can have in your practice besides competence and ethics. You need to know where your clients are being referred from.

If you know who these people are but just do not have a list of the addresses and email information, then you should make that list. If you do not have time to do that, then do a job posting on upwork.com and somebody is going to be willing to do it for $3 to $5 an hour. Just provide the names and they will make you a spreadsheet of the website addresses and all of the contact information.

I know the rate sounds low, but the reality is there are people in other economies of the world to where $3 to $5 an hour is a lot of money. These people, with a little bit of guidance, can get a spreadsheet done that might take you 20 hours and one year to complete. They can do it almost (and sometimes literally) overnight while you sleep. So make that list.

Book marketing strategy #4: Mail to potential referral sources:

Are there people that you want to meet that you think could be a good potential referral relationship? Are you afraid they might question your competence and legitimacy, or just not be interested in meeting?

Then send them a book in the mail. After you do that, wait a week and follow up with a phone call to introduce yourself and coordinate a time to meet. Odds are the person who receives this book from you is probably going to meet with you. Even if initially out of curiosity of meeting somebody who published their own book and sent it to them in the mail.

It is a heck of an icebreaker and a great way to make an introduction. Further, if you are a younger or less experienced therapist, this is a great way to legitimize your expertise. Most people view a published author as somebody who "knows something about something" and this can help you overcome any questions as to why you are somebody they can trust with a referral for a specific issue that you pride yourself in helping clients handle.

Earlier in my law career, my first book served me well in this regard. I had a lot of people I wanted to meet in estate planning and related legal fields that seemed to think a lawyer needed to have gray hair to know what they were doing. I felt confident in my skill set and knew I had the ability to handle the types of cases I was seeking.

The book, in my view, helped me win over a few of the more experienced lawyers. Most of them seemed impressed by the fact that I wrote a book about the types of cases that I personally wanted to be handling. And I think it made it easier for me to establish my law practice at an earlier age than many do. Of course, the board certification I received didn't hurt either, but before I had that, the book in my view, was very helpful to me growing my practice through referral marketing.

Book marketing strategy #5: Make book available for downloading on your website:

Once your book is in the hands of the people that are your clients and your referral sources, one of the next best things you can do to market your book is to get it up on your website, or at least have something on your website to where people can contact you to get the book.

This can be done in a very easy way and there are more sophisticated ways to do it too.

Let's start with the simple. On the homepage of your website, you can reference the fact that you have written a book about whatever the topic is that your clients are interested in. You can put that you are happy to give out a free copy of the book to anyone who requests it. Then just list your email address and instructions for contacting you to request the book. You can choose to send the book by email copy, or you can take it a step further and do what I do and send the book by email to them and offer to send them a hard copy in the mail.

You'll spend a little money on postage and book printing this way, but for my law practice this investment is well worth it. The people who are going to take the time to request a book about something that is important to them are the types of people who have a higher likelihood of being excellent clients.

You can also take this a step further with a few software programs. Through programs like convertkit.com, mailchimp.com, infusionsoft.com, you can set up part of your website to allow you to automatically deliver the books by email to the people who request a copy.

The way it works is illustrated on divorceinformationbooks.com, the link to the download books section of my website. Basically, people enter in their email address and any other contact information you want to designate and click a button. Once they click the button, the program (ConvertKit, MailChimp, Infusionsoft, and many others) will automatically email them a copy of the book, and anything else you want to send them. I use this as part of a more advanced follow-up marketing program that will also email the person who downloads the book with some other information in a "drip marketing" style over a period of time.

Of course, if you're going to be sending emails to people, the ethical thing to do (and what is required by my regulators and probably yours) is to have a disclaimer stating that they will get some follow-up information from you in addition to the book that they can opt out of at any time.

These programs, in my view, are worth the money because they get the books to the people who request them automatically with no effort from you. Most of these programs start in the range of $30 a month. Isn't that worth saving a few hours of your time a month? You can start to get really sophisticated with this and use a program like Infusionsoft which I do, but there's no need to do this to start.

My advice is: keep it simple and just start. You can just have something on the website telling people to email you to get a copy of the book, and you can manually email it to them. There are also many email software platforms you may want to explore utilizing.

A few are MailChimp, ConvertKit, Constant Contact, and Infusionsoft.

Book marketing tip #6: Repurpose the book on your website and marketing materials:

So how many pages is your website? How does that compare to the number of pages in your book? Why is the content in your book not all over your website?

Think about it. Your website is minimal. People find you online. You've written a book. Isn't there something that can be done here?

Yes, there is. Repurpose the content of the book and put it all over your website. If you want to keep it simple, you can literally cut and paste the content from the book and make it the content of a webpage. No one will even know the difference. They will just think you have a huge expansive website and they will never know it is basically all the same stuff in your book. I did this with several of my books on my website, www.brucepa.com. The website now has over 100 pages, most of which is content from the pages of the books that I've written. In some situations, it is the exact same content cut from the Microsoft Word file and pasted onto the web page.

Obviously you want to have a decent looking website. You might need to do a little more than simply copy and paste the words of your book onto a web page. The point here is use the content you have already written and put it up on your webpage and you will have a better web page with more material.

You will also be spreading the message in another format. Some people don't read books. But they read websites. And if they read your website with the content you have written, that helps them solve a very important problem related to their mental health. You will be helping that person. And you can help a lot of people just like that if you put your book content on your website.

Of course, the people who read this content on your website are going to be more likely to call you to help them solve their particular problem if they're looking for a therapist to help them. This is a great way to passively market your practice.

You can also include links in the content (that is basically cut and pasted from your book) stating that you've written a book on this issue that is available for free download. Then you link to where they download the book on your website. This is just a way of making it easier to get people to get your book, which makes it more likely they will call you for an appointment.

Book marketing strategy #7: Market the book through advertisements:

Most of you might not even need to get to this point. But there is a powerful form of marketing called "direct response marketing." With this style of marketing, the intention is to basically market information. Try to get people to "raise their hand" to request more information about services that you offer.

This type of marketing is very helpful when you are offering services (like being a divorce lawyer or marriage counseling therapist) that has a "long buying cycle." For people seeking these types of services, they might research the topic (like marriage counseling or divorce law or personality disorders) a long time before they actually go and get professional help with the issue. This is because they are on the fence about getting the help, or don't even know if they need it yet. Or they are just nervous to talk to anyone.

Through direct response marketing of your book, you bring people to the information they need that makes it more likely for them to learn more about the mental health issues they are looking to solve/ improve, while at the same time helping them understand that you are an expert in that subject area.

Direct response marketing works best with books or other materials that some of the online marketers call "lead magnets." The idea and concept are pretty simple. You do an advertisement that gives people the option to download or request your book as "free information".

Then when people make the request for the information, you send it to them, and if your ethics boards allow it, you periodically send follow-up information. This can all be done through email, using $30 a month programs like ConvertKit or MailChimp (they have free versions too if you have minimal contact lists and are comfortable with fewer features.) And programs like the one I use, Infusionsoft, can do a lot of sophisticated things this way.

So after they receive your information, over a period of time, they receive more helpful information from you, and in an automatic fashion if you use the programs I just mentioned or ones like them. Over time, the idea is that when they reach the point of where they are looking to seek professional help, they are still thinking of you as you were on the "top of their mind" based on the helpful information you've been sending them.

This is the only type of advertising I do in my law practice and it works. You can do these types of advertisements very easily through Google AdWords, through Facebook advertising, and through the other directory services. As an example, a lot of therapists use psychologytoday.com for advertising. You can include on your Psychology Today profile a link a reference to the fact that you have written a book on (whatever the subject is) that is available for free upon request. Then give the instructions for how to do the book request. You are already paying for that Psychology Today listing, why not add this to it?

You can do the same thing through virtually every single way you can think of ever advertising. I think of this type of advertising for my business as serving a dual purpose. First, I am providing a valuable service to the community by giving away information that is very helpful for free. Second, over time, this leads to some of the people who are helped by this information becoming clients of my law firm that are further helped by myself and my client services team.

Again, not everyone will need to get into advertising, but if you're looking to grow your practice further, or fuel a group practice, this can be an excellent strategy.

Next Steps

Just do it. You've written the book. Now it is time to market the book. Pick one of the strategies we have went over and put it into action. Don't get overwhelmed by "analysis paralysis." Pick one of the tactics above that you're most comfortable with and just do it. You are more likely to follow through on a strategy if it is comfortable to you, so don't waste your time and efforts in learning something that does not feel natural to you.

If you take the time to structure the book as we did in part one of this series, and use the tactics in part two of this series to write the book through dictation, you can get to step three covered above and market the book in very little time. You can get this all done within several weeks and less than 20 hours of your time, with probably less than $500 invested if you follow all of the tactics in this series.

HOW TO WRITE A BOOK TO BENEFIT YOUR PRACTICE

I really hope that you consider going through this process. Through writing the book, you will get re-energized in your practice. You will also get more focused on what you can do to be the most help to the clients that you most enjoy serving.

The entire process is a complete win-win. You help do good in the world by putting out valuable information to help people in a time of need. This, in turn, helps bring you more of the people that you take pride in helping into your therapy practice. Which is exactly what you want. Now get writing!

If you have questions about how to get started, please do not hesitate to contact Chris at cbruce@brucepa.com or (561) 810-0170. He is happy to take the time to speak to you to give you some inspiration and guidance.

ABOUT THE AUTHORS

Ashley D. Bruce is a divorce lawyer in West Palm Beach and Wellington, Florida. She got her start in divorce_ from her mother, Bernice Alden Dillman, who practiced divorce and family law for over thirty years in Boca Raton. Growing up Ashley often witnessed clients walk into her mother's office on the first day, distraught, insecure, and upset, and watched them blossom into being more confident, secure, and their knowing that a better life was ahead. Watching her mom guide clients through this transformation helped Ashley realize that she, too, wanted to help clients grow and have a better life.

Asley's early experience shadowing her mother and handling complex business litigation and bankruptcy law (she did a lot of "bet the company" litigation and cases involving financial fraud) was an outstanding platform for the focus of her current law practice, which is handling "the harder" (some might say nasty) divorce and family law cases where something very important or valuable is often at issue.

In all cases, Ashley's goal is to obtain a favorable result for clients as quickly and efficiently as possible so they can move on to the life they desire and deserve to be living. She strongly believes in resolution focused and strategic litigation (which means that she will counsel a client to litigate when it needs to be done, for example to align an unruly spouse more with legal reality when they are taking a ridiculous position) but believes resolving matters out of court is usually in the best interest of the clients, not only financially, but also psychologically.

Outside of the office, and spending time with my her young children, Ashley's passion is animal rescue, and trying to make the world a better place with kindness to animals. Ashley also enjoys horseback riding, mountain biking, snowboarding, tennis, photography, theater, and a variety of other activities. Ashley is married to Christopher R. Bruce, and can be reached at (561) 810-0170 or abruce@brucepa.com.

Christopher R. Bruce is a divorce lawyer and appellate lawyer for divorce cases and has been for nearly all of his legal career and he is a Florida Bar Board Certified Marital & Family Law Specialist. His law practice is predominately limited to representing his South Florida clients in divorce and family court matters involving business valuation and asset tracing issues, the need to confront a difficult or intimidating person, the prosecution or defense of long term financial support claims, or serious issues involving children.

Chris takes a particular interest in representing women in divorces from narcissistic or emotionally abusive/manipulative husbands. This is because Chris feels these cases are most likely to result in his client having a dramatically improved and transformed-for-the-better life once the divorce is over.

Chris founded the Bruce Law Firm, P.A. in November 2016 and the multi-lawyer law firm is limited to divorce and family law matters.

Chris is a native of Palm Beach County, Florida, and a graduate of Palm Beach Gardens High School. Outside of the office, and spending time with his family, his passion is saltwater fishing and marine conservation. Chris enjoys participating in South Florida billfish tournaments and promoting marine species and habitat conservation.

Chris frequently publishes articles on current topics in Florida Divorce Law, and serves as a resource to news agencies reporting on Florida divorce issues. His articles have appeared in the *South Florida Daily Business Review, Palm Beach County Bar Bulletin* and several other Florida Bar publications.

A proponent of keeping families together, Chris developed **www.StayMarriedFlorida.com**, a resource for helping people build, have, and keep happy and healthy relationships.

Chris developed **www.BrucePA.com** to further help people create the best probability for making their divorce a *"Best Divorce"* that allows them to move on to a life to be proud of when their divorce is over. The website's resources include complementary books, seminars, and forums on divorce strategy, law, and procedure.

If you would like to contact Chris in regard to appearing on StayMarriedFlorida.com, a Florida divorce or family law matter, this book, or anything else, you can call (561) 810-0170 or send an email to cbruce@brucepa.com.

Made in the USA
Columbia, SC
16 January 2020